Just for Two

A Collection of 8 Piano Duets in a Variety of Styles and Moods
Specially Written to Inspire, Motivate, and Entertain

DENNIS ALEXANDER

My *Just for You* piano solo collections were some of the first books that I wrote for Alfred Music Publishing Company. They have always been among the top sellers in my library. Now, I am delighted to share with you duet versions of many favorites from those solo books in my new series, *Just for Two*. Piano students always enjoy making music together. I hope that these duets will prove to be "twice the fun" of the original solo versions!

Enjoy, and happy music making.

Dennis Alexander

CONTENTS

Alfred Music
P.O. Box 10003
Van Nuys, CA 91410-0003
alfred.com

ISBN-10: 0-7390-8798-3
ISBN-13: 978-0-7390-8798-5

SOUR LEMONS!
Secondo

Frisky

Dennis Alexander

Both hands one octave lower

SOUR LEMONS!
Primo

Dennis Alexander

Secondo

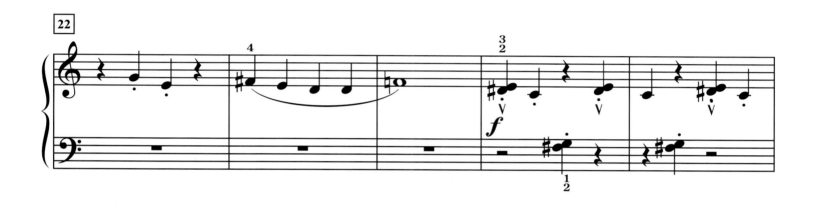

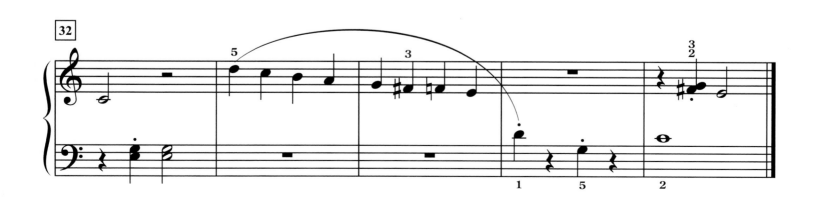

SCOTTISH DANCE
Secondo

Dennis Alexander

SCOTTISH DANCE
Primo

Dennis Alexander

Secondo

CINNAMON POPCORN!
Secondo

Dennis Alexander

Allegro "poppioso"
Both hands as written throughout

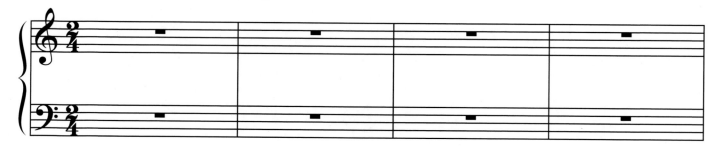

Sempre means "always."

CINNAMON POPCORN!
Primo

Dennis Alexander

Allegro "poppioso"
Both hands TWO octaves higher throughout

* *Sempre* means "always."

Secondo

STROLLING ALONG
Secondo

Dennis Alexander

STROLLING ALONG
Primo

Not too fast
Both hands one octave higher throughout

Dennis Alexander

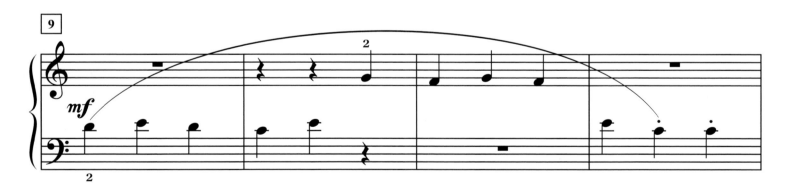

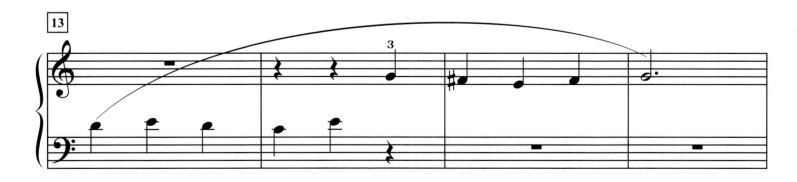

Secondo

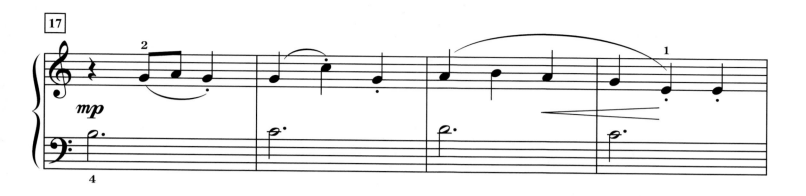

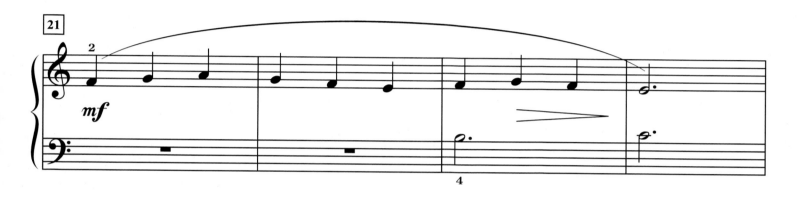

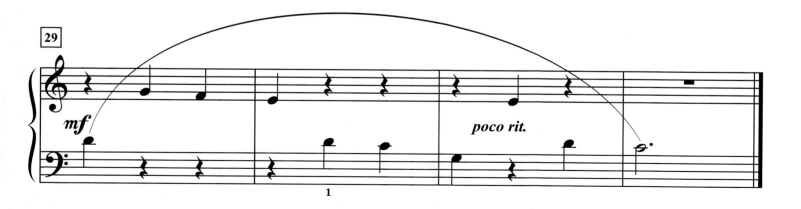

CELEBRATION!
Secondo

Joyfully
Both hands one octave lower throughout

Dennis Alexander

CELEBRATION!
Primo

Dennis Alexander

Joyfully
Both hands one octave higher throughout

Secondo

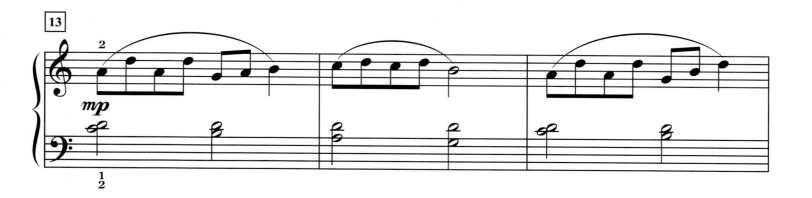

SPOOKS FROM MARS
Secondo

Dennis Alexander

Hauntingly
Both hands one octave lower throughout

SPOOKS FROM MARS
Primo

Dennis Alexander

Secondo

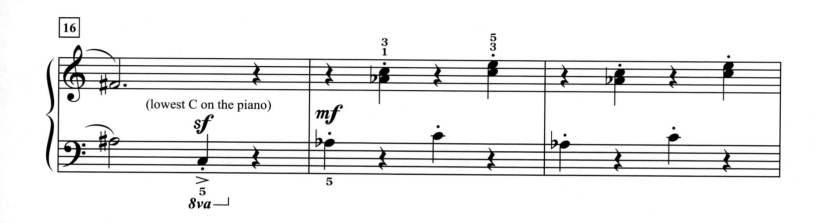

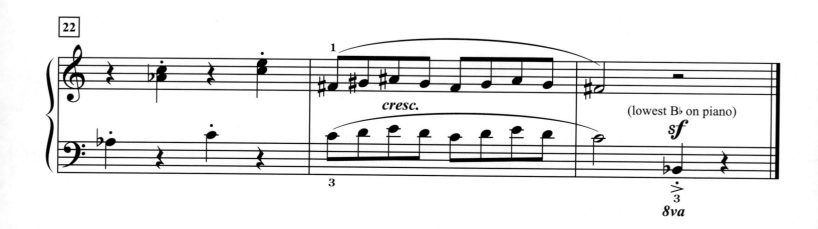

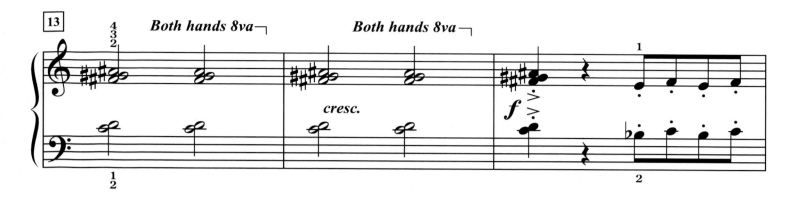

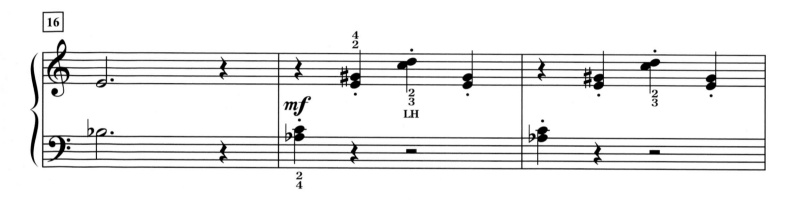

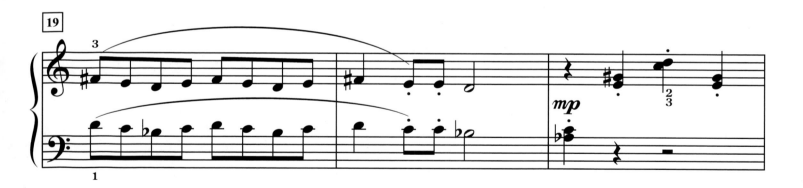

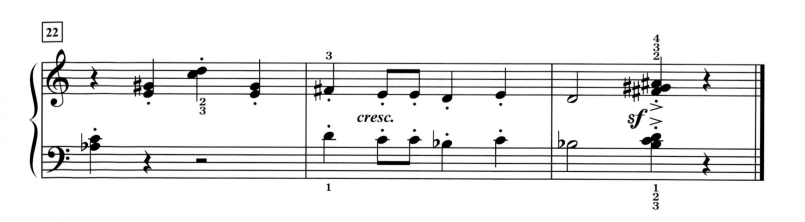

TALLY-HO MARCH
Secondo

Dennis Alexander

Allegro con spirito
Both hands one octave lower throughout

TALLY-HO MARCH
Primo

Dennis Alexander

Allegro con spirito
Both hands one octave higher throughout

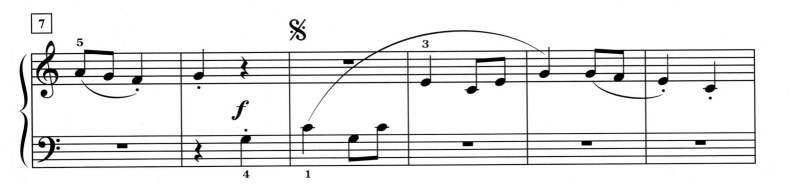

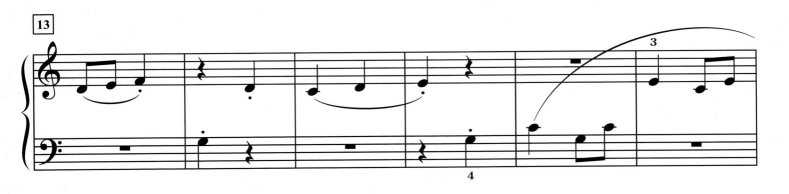

Secondo

DANCE WITH ME
Secondo

Dennis Alexander

DANCE WITH ME
Primo

Moderato

Dennis Alexander

Both hands one octave higher throughout